A-Z SOUTH WALES VALLEYS EAST

D1380363

CONTENTS

REFERENCE

A Road	A467
Under Construction	
Proposed	
B Road	B4251
Dual Carriageway	
One Way Street	→
Traffic flow on A Roads is also indicated by a heavy line on the driver's left.	→
Restricted Access	
Pedestrianized Road	
Track / Footpath	
Residential Walkway	
Railway — Heritage Station, Station, Tunnel, Level Crossing	
Built Up Area	GWENT WAY
Local Authority Boundary	— · — · —
National Park Boundary	
Posttown Boundary	
Postcode Boundary within Posttown	
Map Continuation	32

Car Park selected	P
Church or Chapel	†
Cycleway selected	
Fire Station	■
Hospital	H
House Numbers A & B Roads only	13 8
Information Centre	i
National Grid Reference	³20
Police Station	▲
Post Office	★
Toilet: without facilities for the Disabled	▽
with facilities for the Disabled	▽
Viewpoint	
Educational Establishment	
Hospital or Hospice	
Industrial Building	
Leisure or Recreational Facility	
Place of Interest	
Public Building	
Shopping Centre or Market	
Other Selected Buildings	

SCALE:

1:15,840   4 inches (10.16 cm) to 1 mile,   6.31 cm to 1 kilometre

0	¼	½	¾	1 Mile

0	250	500	750	1 Kilometre

Copyright of Geographers' A-Z Map Company Limited

Head Office:
Fairfield Road, Borough Green, Sevenoaks, Kent TN15 8PP
Telephone: 01732 781000 (Enquiries & Trade Sales)
Telephone: 020 7440 9500 (Retail Sales)
www.a-zmaps.co.uk

Copyright © Geographers' A-Z Map Co. Ltd. 2003

Ordnance Survey® This product includes mapping data licensed from Ordnance Survey® with the permission of the Controller of Her Majesty's Stationery Office.

© Crown Copyright 2003. All rights reserved. Licence number 100017302

Edition 1 2003   Edition 1a 2005 (part revision)

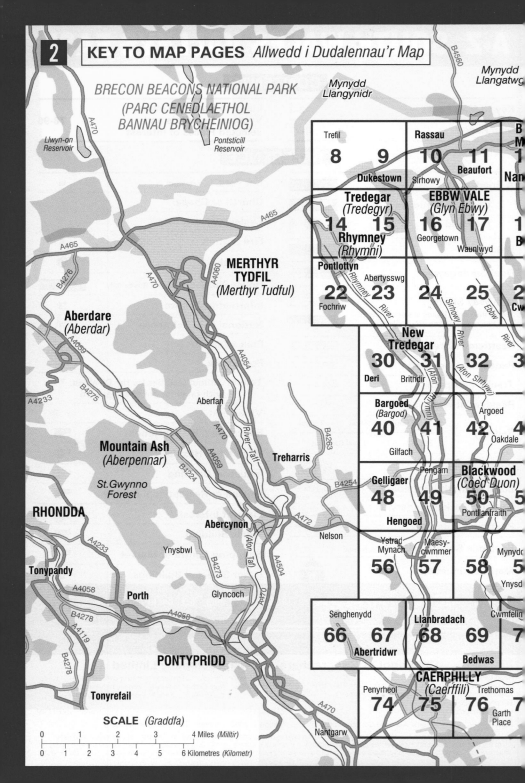

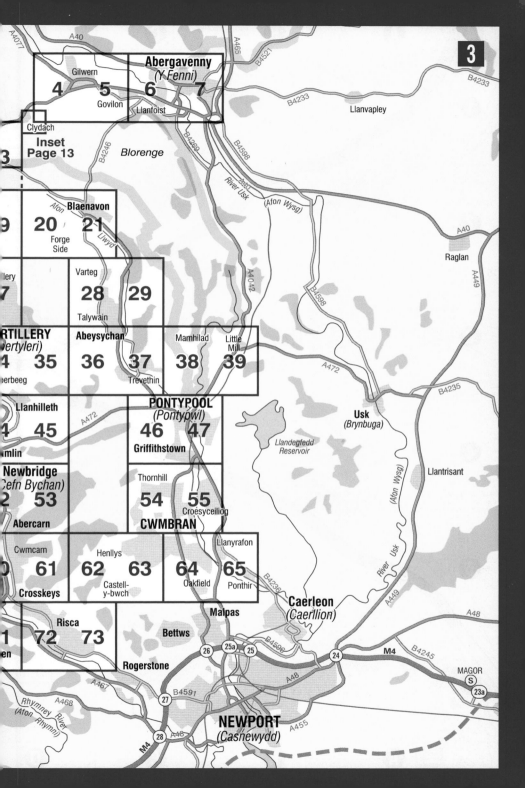

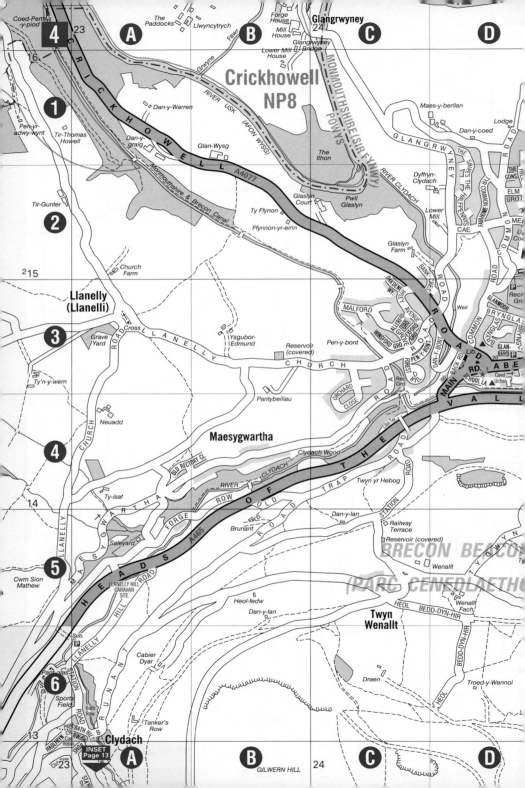

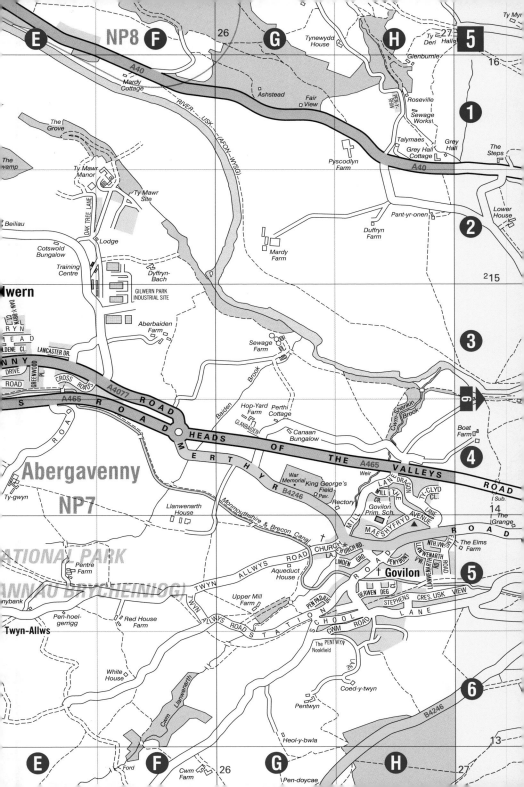

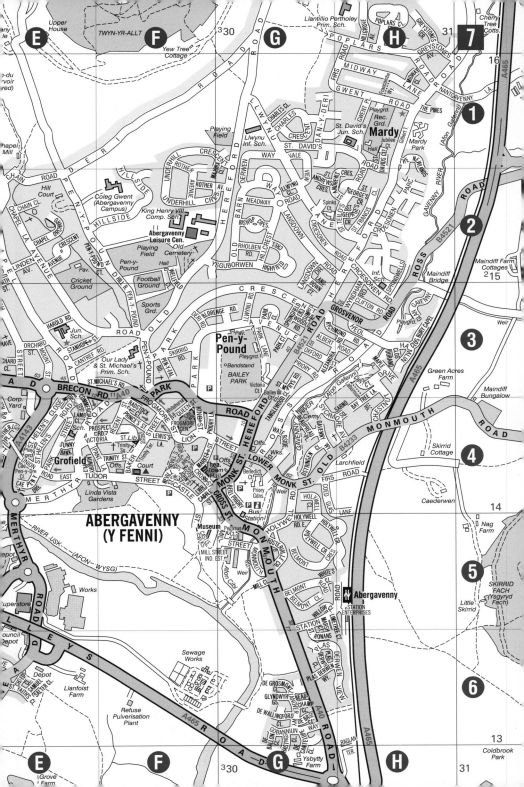

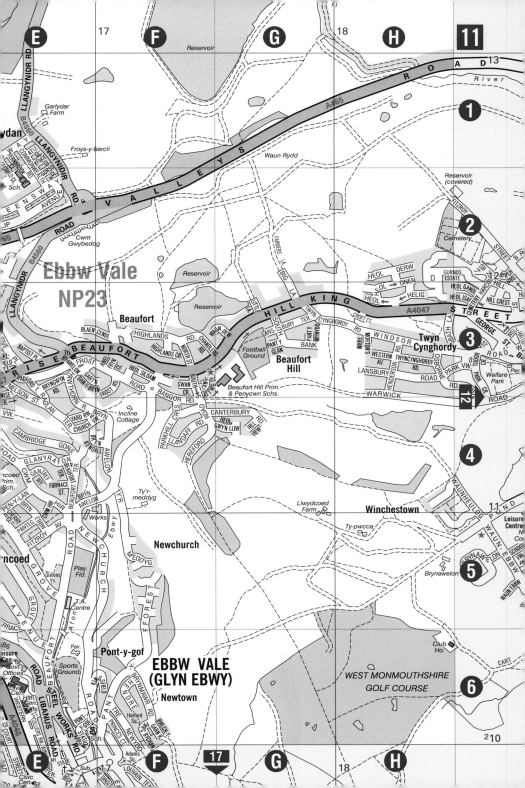

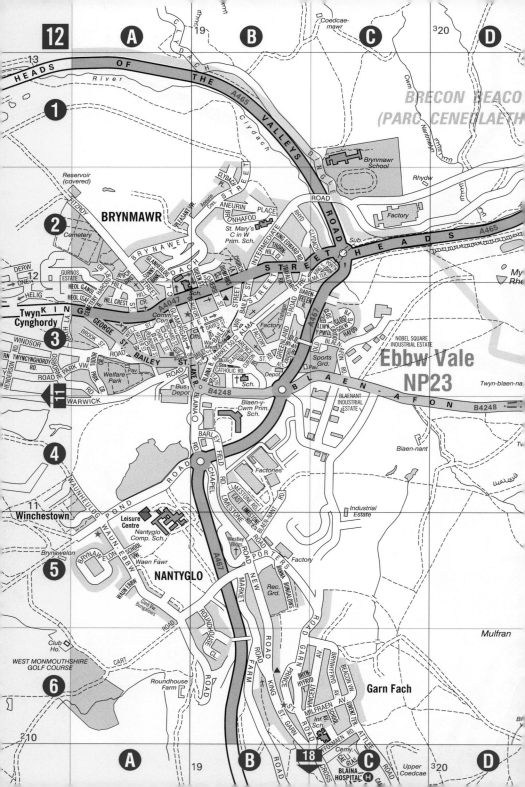

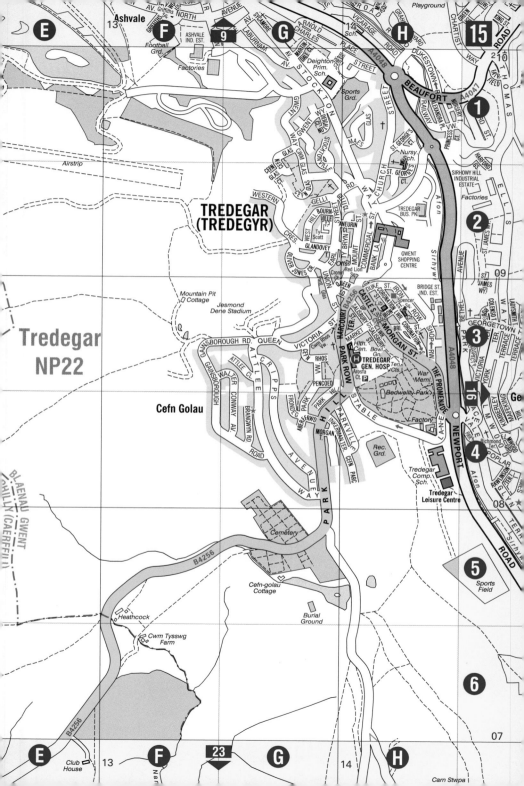

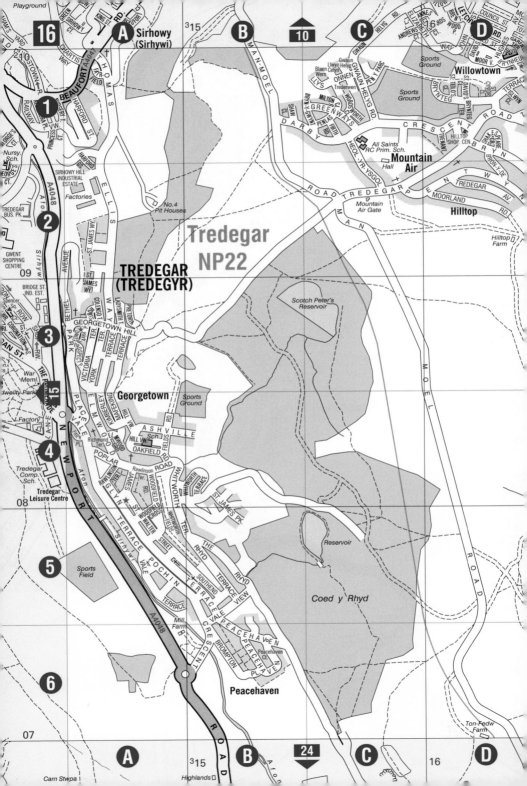

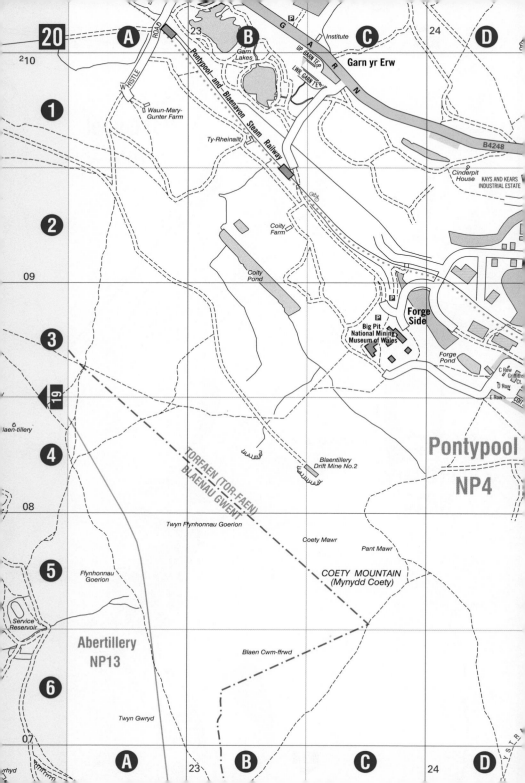

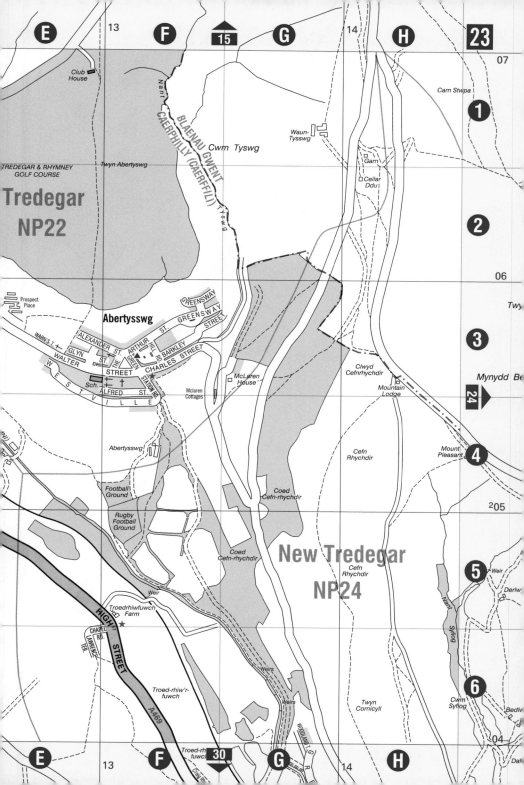

Peacenaven

315 N

16

16

Tor Farm M

07

A

B

C

D

Carn Stwpa

Highlands

Hunt's Lodge

Troedrhiw-gwair

1

SIRHOWY VALLEY

Coronation Villas

Trial Level

Bedwellty Pits

Sirhywi

Afon

A4048

Railway Houses

2

06

Twyn Yr Hyddod

Tredegar NP22

Lower Farm

Darren Cruglwyn

3

Mynydd Bedwellte

23

4

Mount Pleasant

Darren Ddu

05

Pochin Houses

Fed

5

Weir

Derlwyn

Nant Syfiog

BLAENAU GWENT

CAERPHILLY (CAERFFILI)

New Tredegar NP24

6

Cwm Syfiog

Bedlwyn

A4048

R

04

A

B

31

C

D

315

16

Pen-rhiw gwaith

Ty'r Cwrt

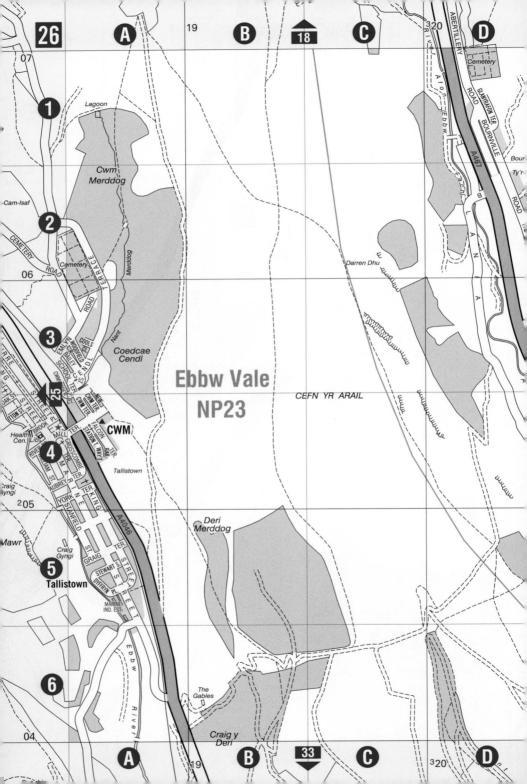

A 19 B 18 C 320 D

1

Ebbw Vale

NP23

CEFN YR ARAIL

CWM

Tallistown

Deri
Merddog

5
Tallistown

6

Lagoon

Cwm
Merddog

Cemetery

Coedcae
Cendl

Darren Dhu

Cemetery

ABERTILLERY

BOURNVILLE

Craig
Gyngi

The
Gables

Craig y
Deri

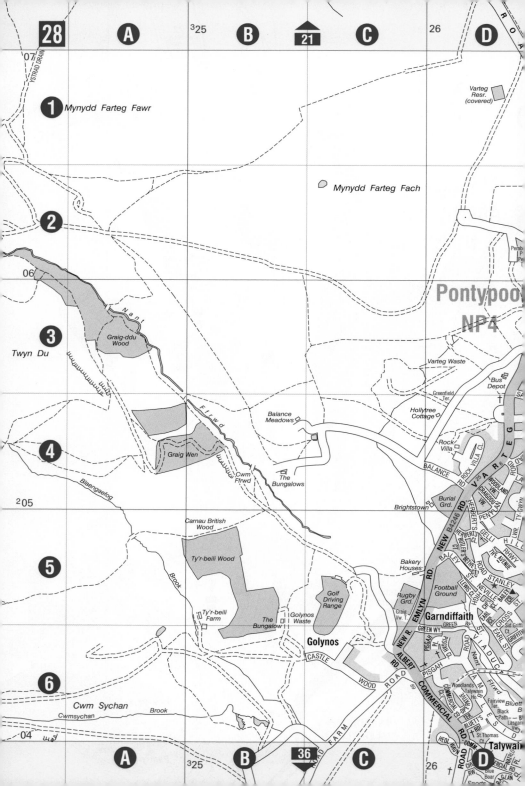

07
YSTRAD DRAIN

1 Mynydd Farteg Fawr

Varteg
Resr.
(covered)

Mynydd Farteg Fach

2

06

Nant

Pontypool
NP4

Graig-ddu
Wood

3

Twyn Du

Varteg Waste

Bus
Depot

Greenfield
Ter.

Hollytree
Cottage

Ffrwd

Balance
Meadows

Rock
Villa

4

Graig Wen

BALANCE

ROCK VILLA CL.

Cwm
Ffrwd

The
Bungalows

Brightstown

Burial
Grd.

Blaengaefog

²05

NEW B4246 ROAD

HERBERT'S CT.

PENYLAN

Carnau British
Wood

Bakery
Houses

Ty'r-beili Wood

5

Football
Ground

Rugby
Grd.

Golf
Driving
Range

Graig
Ww. T.

Garndiffaith

GREEN WY.

Brook

Ty'r-beili
Farm

The
Bungalow

Golynos
Waste

Golynos

CASTLE

NEW R.

ALBERT

PISGAH

6

WOOD

ROAD

COMMERCIAL

Woodlands
Ter.

Talywain Ho.

Fairview
Ter.

Bluett
Black

Cwm Sychan

Cwmsychan

Brook

St. Thomas

Talywain

04

Blue
Boar

E · Ty Michael Farm · Cwmavon Reservoir · 27

F

G

28

H

BRECON BEACONS
NATIONAL PARK
(PARC CENEDLAETHOL
BANNAU BRYCHEINIOG)

MONMOUTHSHIRE (SIR FYNWY)

TORFAEN (TOR-FAEN)

Garn-llech

1

Gallowsgreen

FURLONG
WOOD

Pwll Gwyn

Cwmavon
Ho.

Forge
Row

2

Mynydd Garnclochdy

Garn Clochdy

06

Works

Cwmavon

Pistyll-gwyn

LLANOVER R.

Penrhoel-
Medwyn

Kear's
Row

Beili-glas

Craig y Felin

Varteg

Hafod-
wenog

3

Little Beili-glas

Lower
Little Beili-glas

Beili-glas

Ty Dda
Farm

PENY FELDS

Bryn-glas

4

Mill Farm

Pen-y-lan Wood

Hen-felin

Coedcae
Sai

05

Cwmavon
Farm

Pen-y-ddoyga

Rec.
Grd.

Pant-y-gelli

Maelor

Pant-yr-heol

5

Garnteg
Primary
Sch.

Greenmeadow
Farm

Nant-yr-mailor
Reservoir

Cwm
Lasgarn

Nant

Garn-wen

6

Rising Sun
Bridge

ABERSYCHAN

LASGARN
WOOD

Victoria
Village

E · 27

F

37

G

28 LASGARN

H

04

LANE

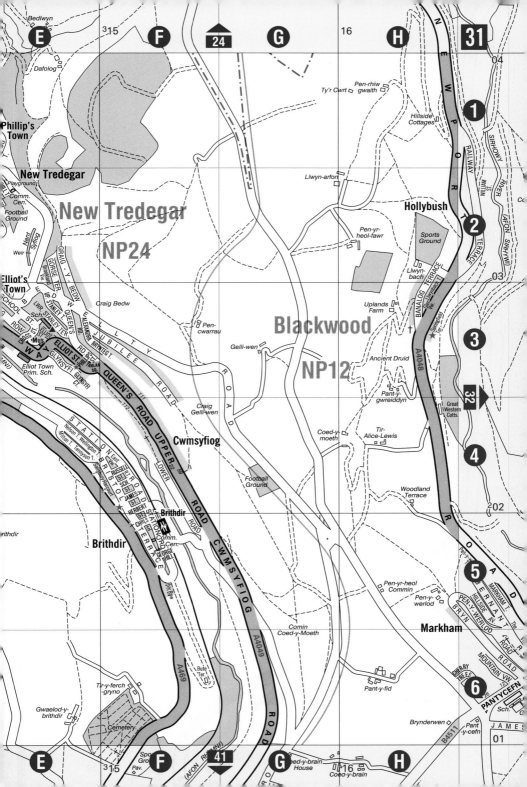

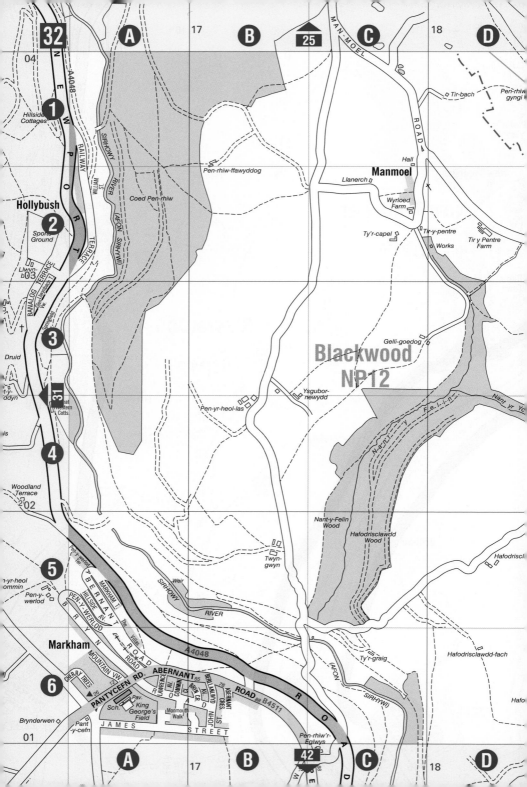

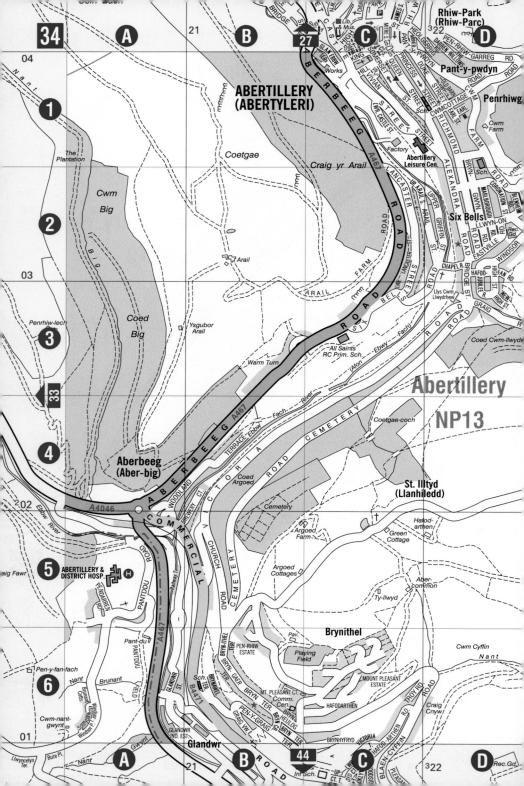

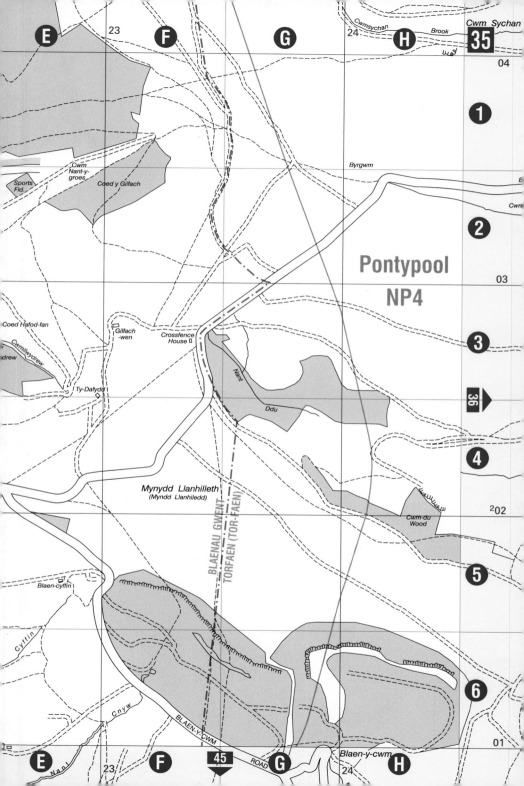

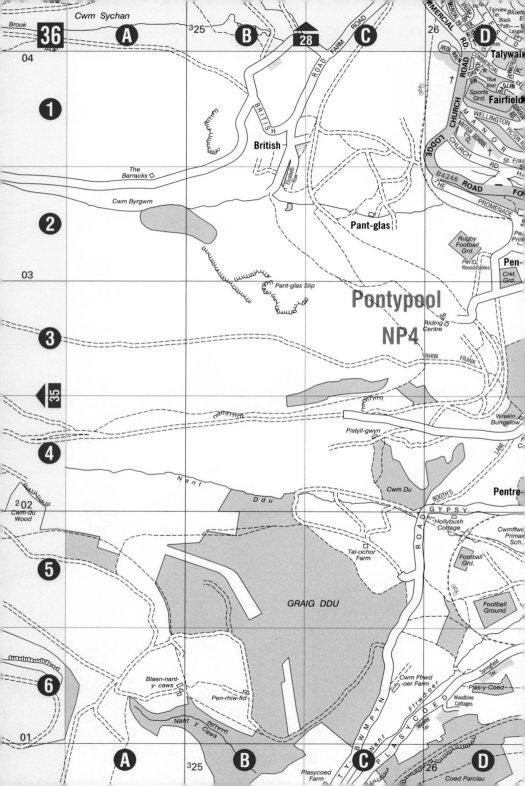

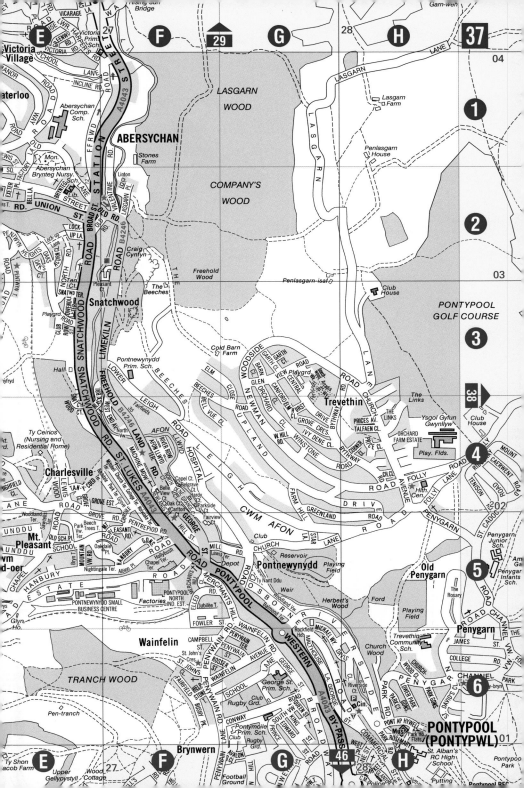

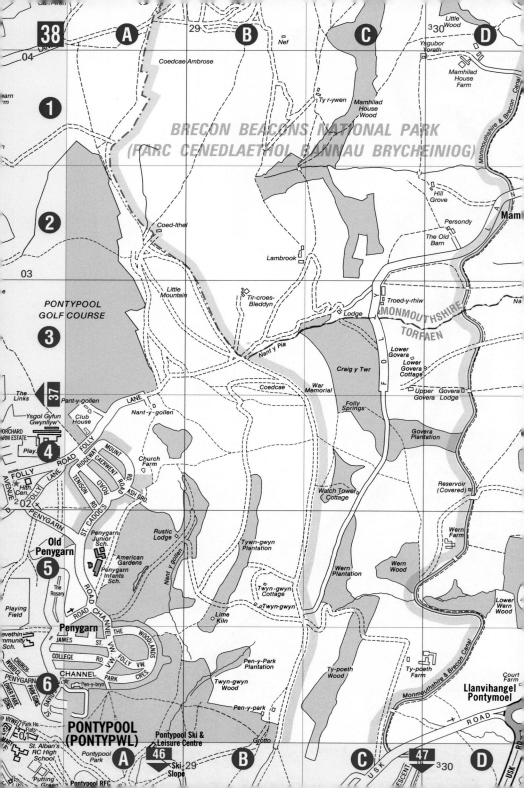

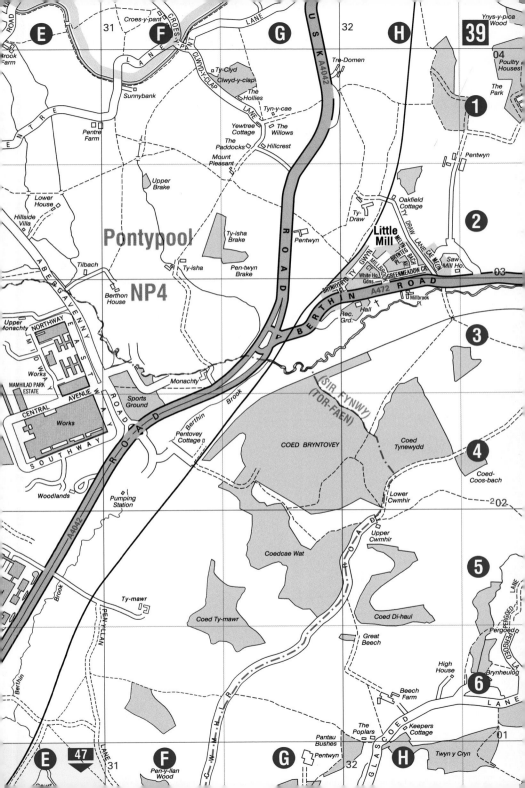

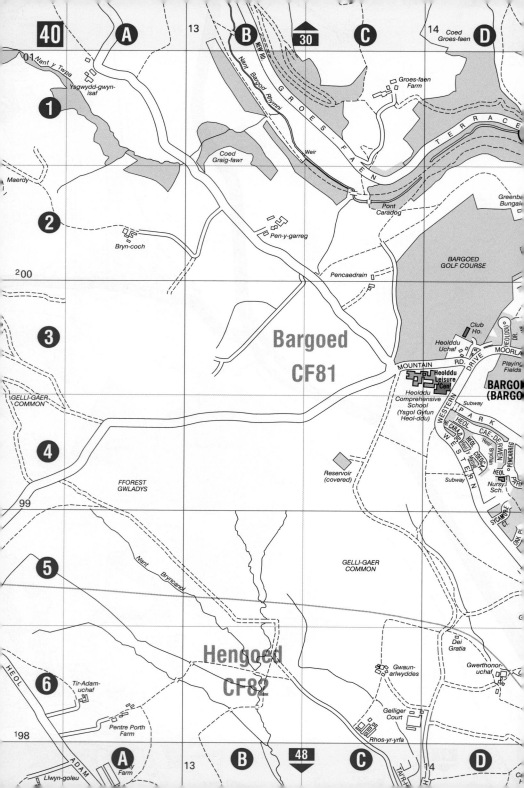

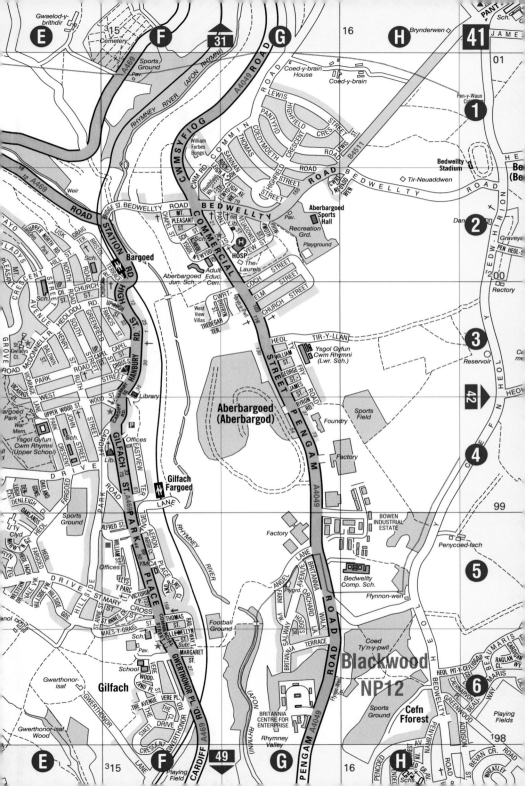

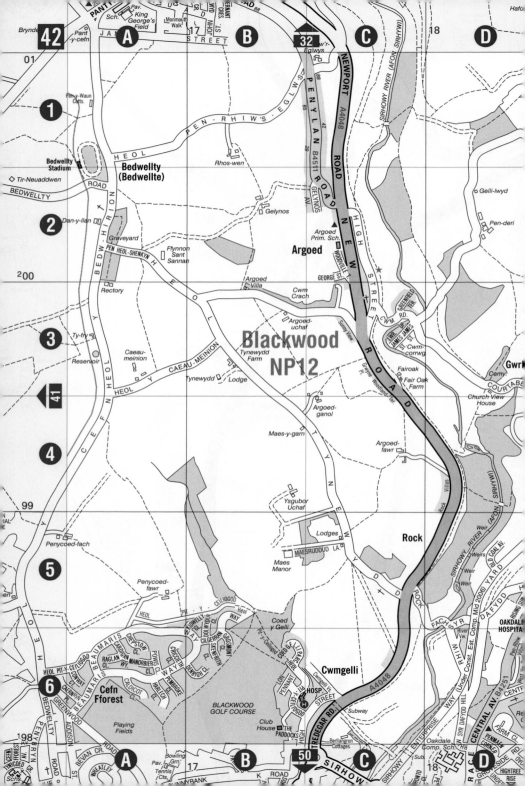

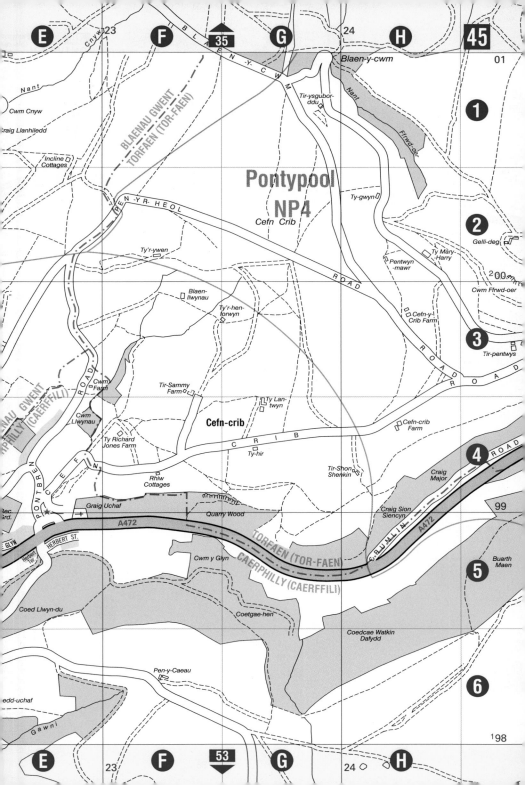

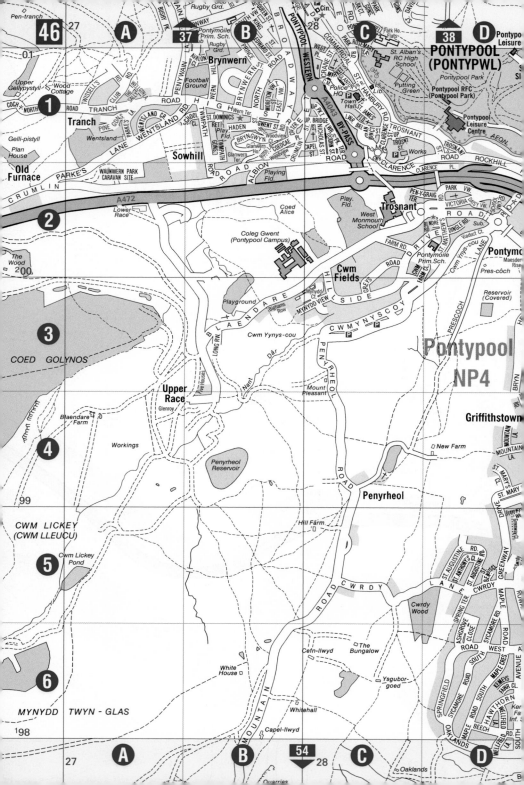

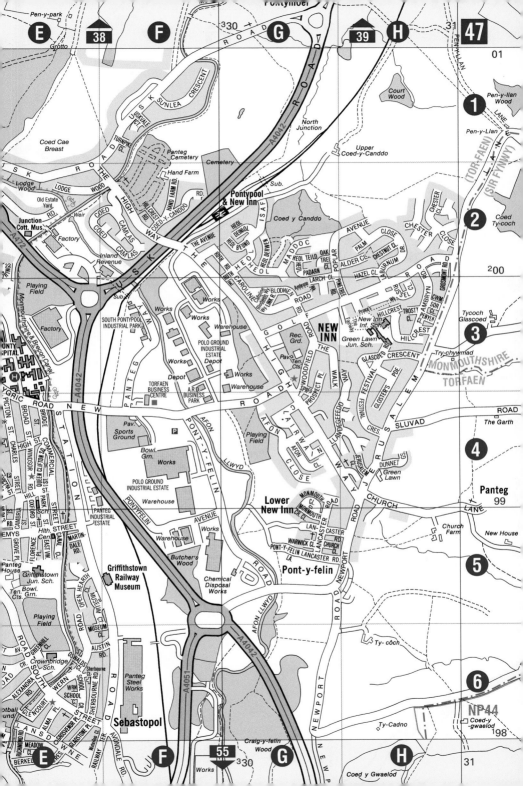

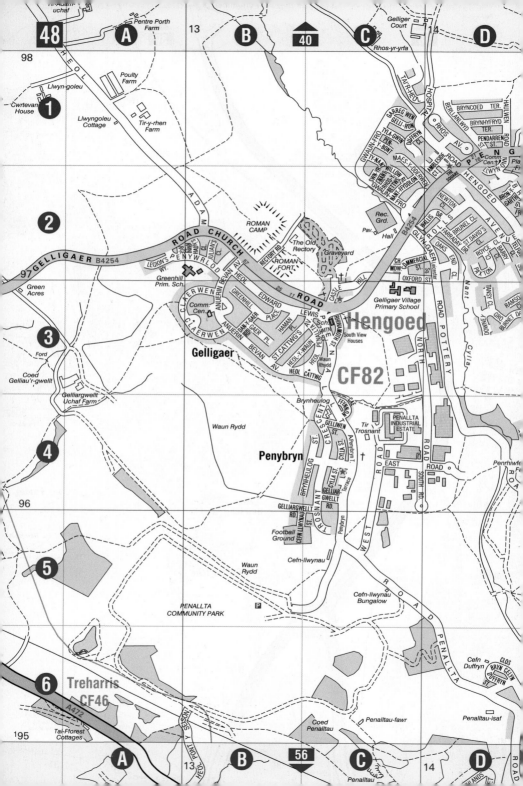

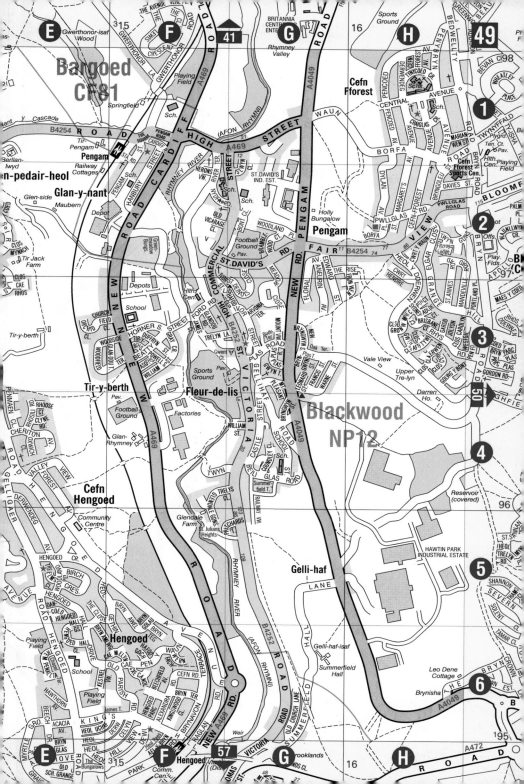

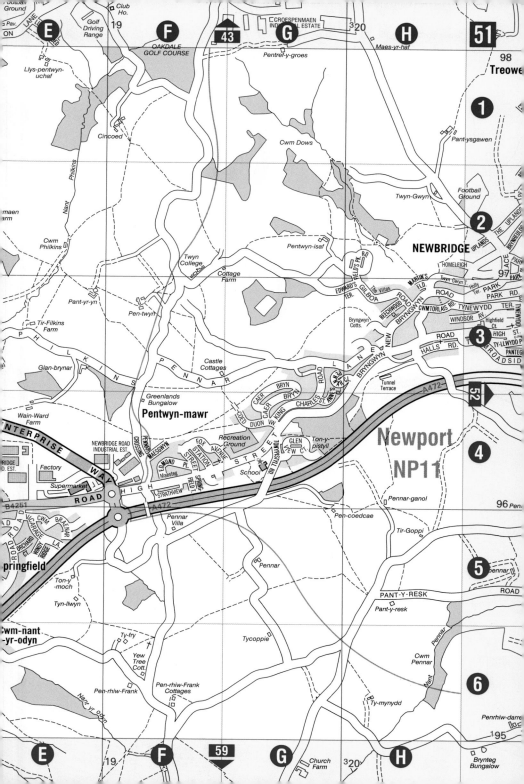

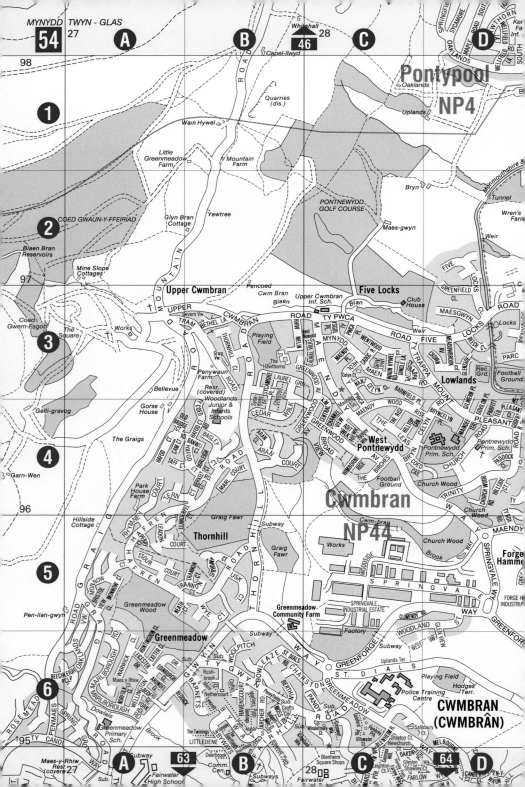

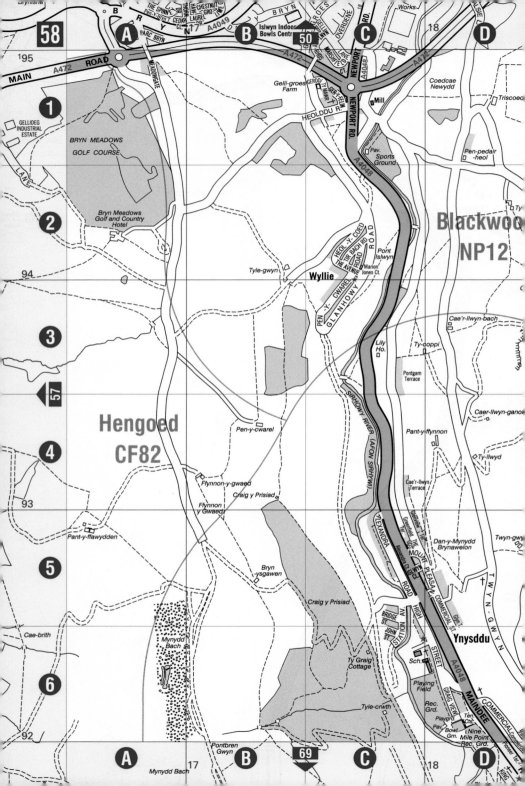

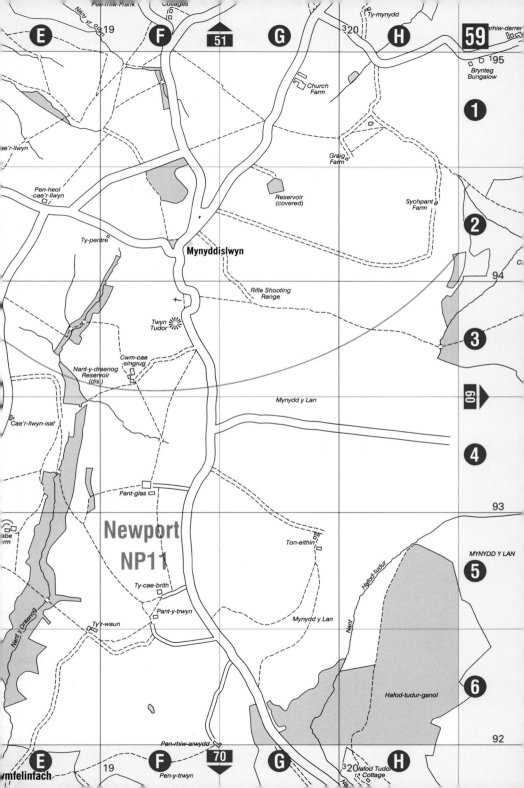

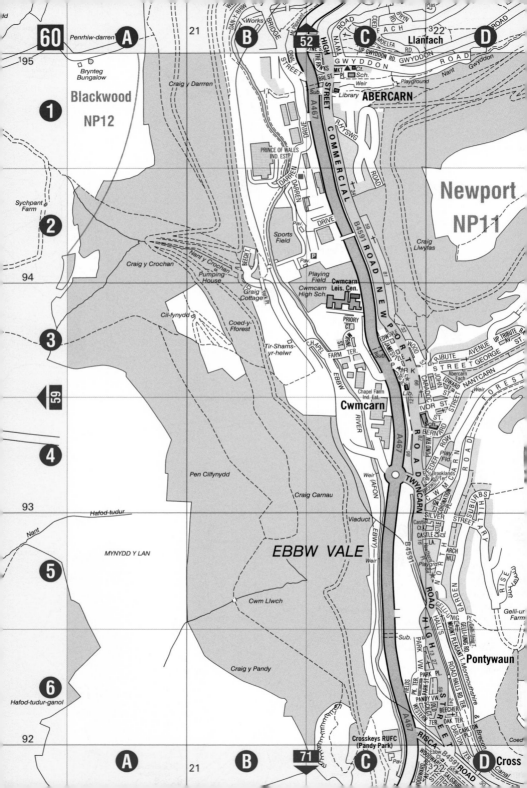

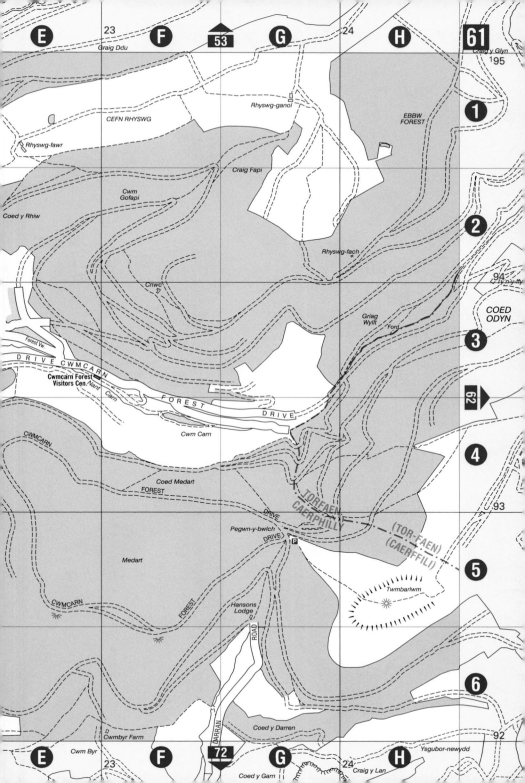

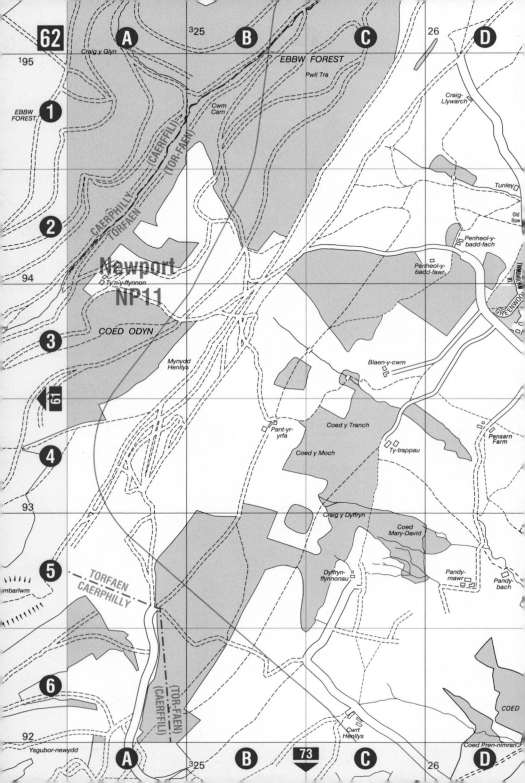

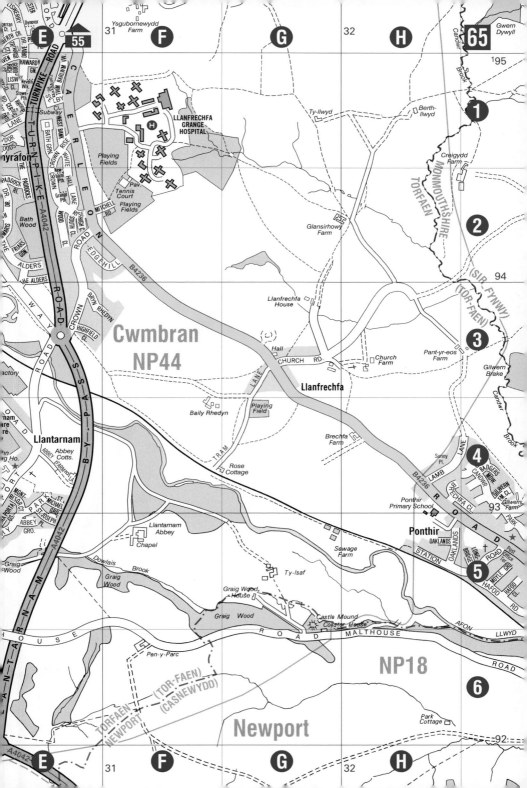

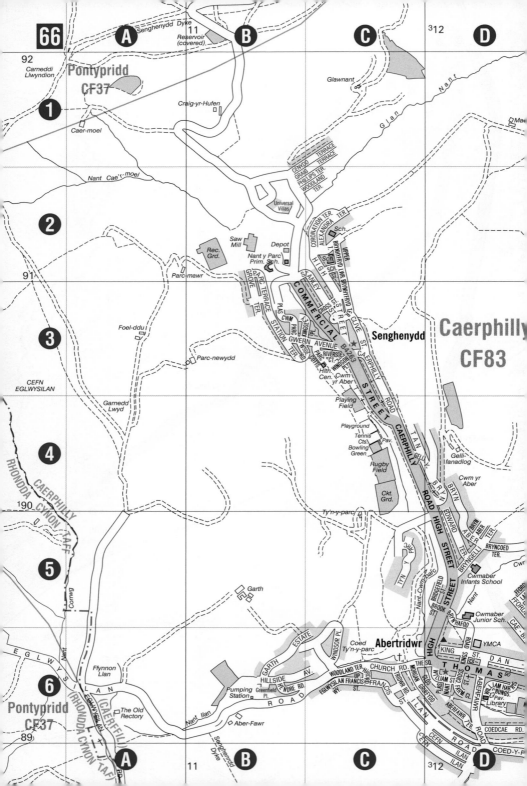

A   B   C   D

Senghenydd Dyke
Reservoir
(covered)

11

**Pontypridd
CF37**

Carneddi
Llwyndion

1

Craig-yr-Hufen

Caer-moel

Glawnant

Nant

Nant Cae'-moel

Glan

GENFOD TERRACE
GRAIG TERRACE
PHILLIPS TER.
WOODLAND
TER.

2

Universal
Villas

CORONATION TER.

ALEXANDRA TER.

Sch.

Saw
Mill

Rec.
Grd.

Depot

Nant y Parc
Prim. Sch.

BRYNHYFRYD LWR
BRYNHYFRYD UPR.

HIGH

UPPER

Sch.

91

Parc-mawr

PARC TERRACE

GROVE

STANLEY

CROSS STREET

PLAS

COMMERCIAL

CLIVE ST.

Senghenydd

**Caerphilly
CF83**

3

Foel-ddu

Parc-newydd

STATION TER.

TER.

GWERN

CWM
PARC

AVENUE B4263

RIVERSIDE
CT.

WINDSOR
PL.

Hlth.
Cen.

Cwm
yr Aber

CAERPHILLY ROAD

STREET

CAERPHILLY

ROAD

CEFN
EGLWYSILAN

Garnedd
Lwyd

Playing
Field

Playground

Tennis
Cts

Pav.

Bowling
Green

Rugby
Field

Gelli-
ifanadlog

Cwm yr
Aber

GELLI

BRYN

LAN

4

**RHONDDA
CYNON TAFF**

CAERPHILLY

Ckt.
Grd.

BRYN EDWARD

BRYN ABER ABEL

190

Ty'n-y-parc

HIGH STREET

BRYNGELLI

BRYNCOED
TER.

5

Cornwg

Nant

Garth

TYN

Nant-Cwm-parc

Bridgefield

BROOK

Cwmaber
Infants School

Cwr

6

**Pontypridd
CF37**

89

Flynnon
Llan

The Old
Rectory

Pumping
Station

Greenfield
PL.

HILLSIDE

LYNDRE RD.

AV.

GARTH ESTATE

WINDSOR PL.

ROAD

Coed
Ty'n-y-parc

Abertridwr

WOODLAND TER.

EGLWYSILAN

UP.

FRANCIS
WY.

CHURCH RD.

FRANCIS
ST.

TRWYN RD.

MORGAN

BRIDGFORD

THE SQ.

THOMAS

KING ST.

WILLIAM ST.

GWAS. GOS.

DAN

ST.

JAM HAR'S
BUNGS.

Pav.
Library

YMCA

Cwmaber
Junior Sch.

RHAFOD ROAD

ABERFAWR

ABERFAWR TER.

CAE FFLORDD

FFLORDD

COEDCAE RD.

CEFN
ILAN

ILAN ROAD

COED-Y-P

Nant Ilan

Aber-Fawr

Senghenydd
Dyke

EGLWYSILAN
(RHONDDA CYNON TAF)
(CAERPHILLY)

Nant

RHONDDA CYNON TAF
CAERPHILLY

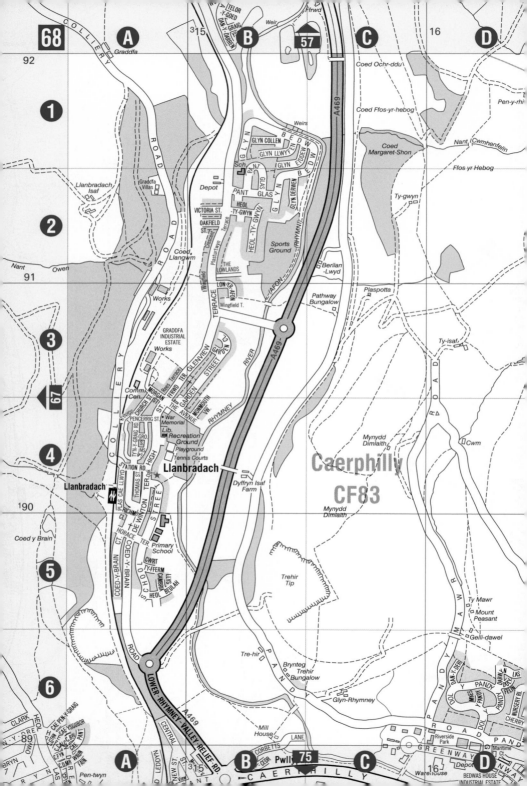

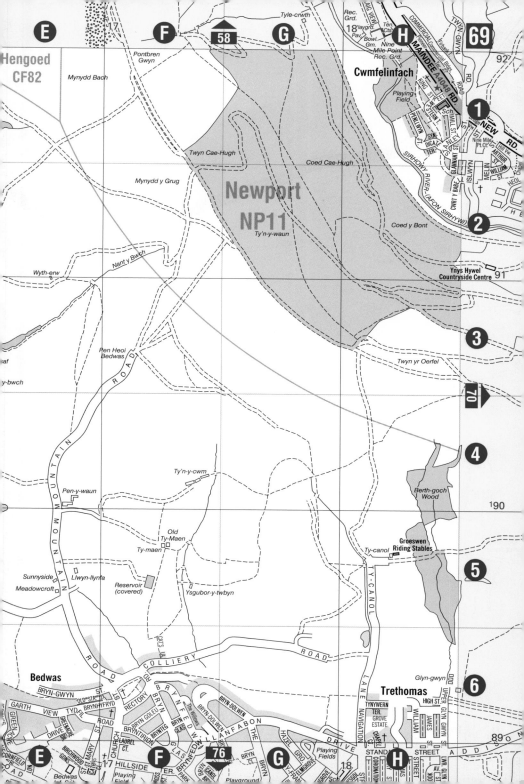

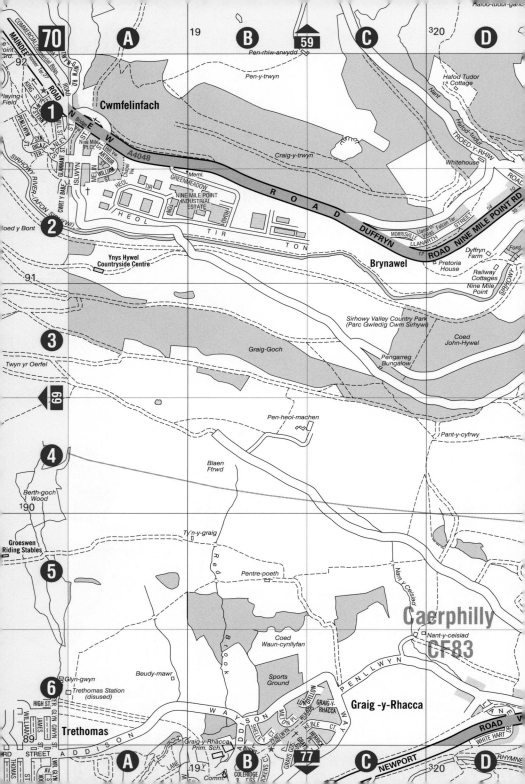

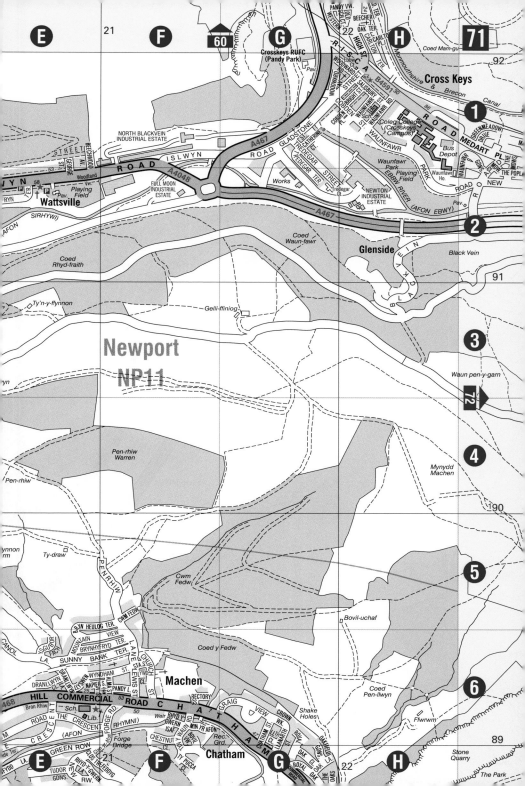